The Little Society of St. Rita
Prayer Book

NIHIL OBSTAT: J. Brian Bransfield. S.T.D.
IMPRIMATUR: + Charles J. Chaput, O.F.M. Cap
Archbishop of Philadelphia

Bee image from http://www.antiqueimages.blogspot.com

Front cover photo from an old prayer card reprinted
by St. Benedict Press

Back cover photo by Nacia Ruszak
Photo on page 8 by Adele Ruszak
Quote on back cover from *The Precious Pearl, The Story of Saint
Rita of Cascia* by Michael Di Gregorio, OSA

Produced by Not Forgotten Publishing Services
NotForgottenPublishing@gmail.com
Available at https://www.createspace.com/4368347
and at Amazon.com
Printed in the United States of America

Contents

Foreword

THE IMITATION OF JESUS and the faithful observance of his Gospel have been the aspiration of untold numbers of men, women, and children for 2,000 years. Some of the paths that individuals have followed to reach these two ends have become so popular and effective as to be recognized as trustworthy spiritualities of the Christian tradition. Saints such as Augustine, Dominic, Francis, and Ignatius are but a few of the great spiritual masters who have outlined approaches to Gospel life that have enabled sincere Christians to "put on the Lord Jesus Christ" and so pursue the path of holiness.

This little booklet presents elements of an approach to Gospel living based on the life and spiritual practices of Saint Rita of Cascia, herself a disciple of Saint Augustine. Her vocation was, in successive moments, that of wife, mother, widow, and finally, for forty years, an Augustinian Nun.

Though she lived many centuries ago, in a society and culture far different from our own, Saint Rita's devotion to Christ and the choices she made in fidelity to his Gospel still speak powerfully to people of today, offering valuable testimony to the possibility of seeking and attaining holiness in daily life.

The Little Society of Saint Rita offers the example of the Saint of Cascia especially to young women who seek responsible guidance and spiritual companionship in living their Christian faith. Through the practice of prayer, reflection, and discussion with like-minded fellow believers, and by following the values and virtues exhibited by their patroness, young disciples of Christ will find encouragement and inspiration in living the Gospel with joyful enthusiasm.

A word of acknowledgment and appreciation is due to Janice Russoniello, who conceived this Society under the protection and intercession of Saint Rita and brought it to its present state of development. May this little book, also the product of her efforts, guide the Society's growth and enrich the lives of its members with an eager desire to live the Gospel of Christ ever more faithfully. May Saint Rita herself obtain God's blessings on this initiative and on all those who enter upon it.

Fr. Michael Di Gregorio, O.S.A.

But whoever obeys me dwells in security,
in peace, without fear of harm.

Proverbs 1:33

Introduction

DEAR CLIENT OF ST. RITA,

In today's world we hear so much about the empowerment of women. The focus of this empowerment often tends to be self-centered and worldly.

The Little Society of St. Rita seeks a different kind of empowerment; through the constant request for the intercessory prayer of St. Rita of Cascia (for growth in virtue, fulfillment of God's will, and guidance in our vocational choices) we will welcome God to act in our lives.

Our beloved St. Rita lived every vocation. She was a wife and mother, a single Catholic laywoman making her way in the world, and a consecrated religious sister. By God's grace she lived each of these vocations in an exemplary way, a way most worthy of imitation. St. Rita, through these gifts of grace, became a peacemaker within her family and community. She became a model for others in how to forgive and truly reconcile when faced with adversity and conflict.

Dearest Client, put yourself under the patronage of this powerful saint, that you may become like St. Rita: a precious pearl before God.

Guidelines

for Creation of a Little Society of St. Rita

THE LITTLE SOCIETY OF ST. RITA promotes and facilitates a period of formation for young Catholic women under the patronage of St. Rita of Cascia. It is dedicated to forming young women to be holy Catholic women: wives and mothers, single laywomen, and consecrated religious sisters. The main focus of this society is the constant request for the intercessory prayers of St. Rita for growth in virtue, fulfillment of God's will, and guidance in vocational choices.

Members of the Little Society of St. Rita should always strive to live in imitation of our beloved patroness. St. Rita lived a hidden life: within her home as wife and mother, within her community as a peacemaker, and within the walls of St. Mary Magdalene Convent in prayer. In her hiddenness, St. Rita performed many simple acts of charity throughout her life and forgave those who had caused her injury.

Members should receive the Holy Sacraments frequently, spend time regularly in Adoration, read about the life of St. Rita (recommended: *The Precious Pearl: The Story of St. Rita of Cascia* by Michael Di Gregorio, O.S.A.), and recite the daily prayers of the Little Society.

 Set times for the group to meet on the same day each month (for instance, each first Saturday) for 9 consecutive months or for 12 consecutive months if adding the Triduum.

 The Novena of St. Rita is recited September through May. If the Triduum is added, it may be recited in June, July, and August.

 During each meeting, members attend Mass together.

 After Mass, members pray the Joyful Mysteries of the Rosary, the Litany of St. Rita, and the Novena Prayers of St. Rita (or Triduum in

Honor of St. Rita during the months of June, July, and August).

 The young women wear a St. Rita medal (available at www.saintritashrine.org) as an outward sign of membership.

 The meetings consist of prayer as well as discussion of the month's virtue and how to live this virtue.

Levels of Formation

First Level of Formation

 Learning to live a life filled with the Sacraments.

 Learning how Our Lady teaches us to live in the Joyful Mysteries and receive the Gifts of God.

 Learning the nine virtues of St. Rita: the gift of prayer, humility, submission to the will of God, obedience, patience, love of Christ's Passion, forgiveness, devotion to the Holy Eucharist, and loving God with our whole heart.

 Discussing what it means to live these virtues and how we apply them to our lives.

 Discussing how to be peacemakers, starting in our own hearts and then with family. Taking time for prayer to allow God to speak to our hearts so that we can radiate peace by first instilling peace within ourselves, and then within our families.

Second Level of Formation

 Continuing to discuss the virtues of St. Rita.

 Discussing Christian duty and peacemaking within the broader community outside the family through the act of hospitality.

Third Level of Formation

 Continuing to discuss the virtues of St. Rita and peacemaking and service to the world.

 Discussing what it means to live as a contradiction.

 Learning how we can discern the will of God in our lives.

The Joyful Mysteries

OUR LADY TEACHES US how to live in the Joyful Mysteries of the Rosary.

The Annunciation

Mary receives Jesus in humility: "Behold the handmaid of the Lord." To God she says yes entirely, not "Yes, but this is what I want." She says to the Angel, "Be it done unto me according to your word." She receives with complete openness what God desires to give her.

How can we receive Jesus with complete openness in the Eucharist?

The Visitation

Mary shares Jesus. She "makes haste to the hill country of Judea." Arriving, she speaks the words of greeting to Elizabeth, and the Holy Spirit is communicated to Elizabeth and to the child in her womb, St. John the Baptist.

How can we make haste to share Jesus with others by our love?

The Nativity

Mary receives the fullness of God's promise spoken by the angel that she would "bear a son and name him Jesus." She ponders this in her heart and marvels at God's abundant gift that she should be the Mother of God.

How do we ponder in our hearts the goodness of God? Do we marvel at the abundant gifts God has given us?

The Presentation

Mary presents Jesus at the temple. After she receives the fullness of God's promise, she presents Jesus to God. She offers God to God.

How do we use God's abundant gifts? Do we return God's abundant gifts to God by sharing with others our talent, treasure, and time?

Mary Finds Jesus in the Temple

Mary, through no fault of her own, becomes separated from Jesus. She and St. Joseph search for Him with longing and desire until they find Him in the temple.

Do we search with longing and desire when we become separated from Jesus? Do we remember where He can always be found?

Daily Prayers
of the Little Society of St. Rita

Mary, Mother Most Pure, *pray for us.*
For purity of mind (in our thoughts), *Hail Mary. . . .*
For purity of body (in our actions), *Hail Mary. . . .*
For purity of heart (in our intentions), *Hail Mary. . . .*

A Prayer for Peace

God of Mercy, give us peace. Peace in our hearts,
peace in our homes, peace in our communities,
peace in the world. *Amen.*

Prayer to Know One's Vocation

O Glorious St. Rita, to whose guiding care I have
committed myself, in this, the most serious affair of
my life, come to my assistance. Obtain for me,
from the crucified Savior the grace to walk only in
that way which He has decreed shall be the means

to the end for which I was created, the enjoyment of God in heaven. *Amen.*

Triduum in Honor of St. Rita

First Day

Rosary of the Blessed Virgin

Prayer:

Direct, we beseech You, O Lord, all our actions by Your holy inspirations, and carry them on by Your gracious assistance, that every prayer and other good work of ours may begin always from You, and by You be happily ended: through Christ our Lord. *Amen.*

O blessed Rita, I take you this day for my special protectress and advocate with God. In all humility I rejoice with you, because you were chosen by God for the special marks of His favors. Obtain for me, by your prayers, a spirit of true courage in all the trials of this life. Make it your special care,

O blessed advocate, to obtain for me an efficacious love of God, a strong love, a pure love, enabling me to surmount all difficulties that might hinder my union with God in life, so that I may become one with Him forever after death.

O glorified Rita, look down upon me still exiled and send me hope and consolation. Obtain for me the grace of imitating your virtues; and if it be God's Holy Will, I beg of you to add your prayers to mine for the obtaining of this, my special request [mention your request].

O Glorious St. Rita, who did miraculously participate in the sorrowful Passion of our Lord Jesus Christ, obtain for me the grace to suffer with resignation the troubles of this life, and protect me in all my needs. *Amen.*

Three each: Our Father, Hail Mary, Glory be.

Second Day

Rosary of the Blessed Virgin

Prayer:

Direct, we beseech You. . . . [as on first day].

O glorious Rita, you who, while on Earth, were a mirror of innocence and a model of penance, O saintly heroine, specially chosen by God to wear on your heart and brow the marks of His love and Passion, look down from Heaven graciously upon my soul and hear my prayers. Obtain for me such a love for Jesus' suffering that ever meditating on His Passion I may make His suffering mine; that I may draw from the wounds of my Savior, as from so many founts of salvation, the grace of lamenting my sins and a firm will to imitate you in penance, if I have not followed you in innocence.

O glorified Rita, look down upon me still exiled and send me hope and consolation. Obtain for me the grace of imitating your virtues; and if it be God's Holy Will, I beg of you to add your prayers to mine for the obtaining of this, my special request [mention your request].

O Glorious St. Rita, who did miraculously participate in the sorrowful Passion of our Lord Jesus Christ, obtain for me the grace to suffer with resignation the troubles of this life, and protect me in all my needs. *Amen.*

Three each: Our Father, Hail Mary, Glory be.

Third Day

Rosary of the Blessed Virgin

Prayer:

Direct, we beseech You. . . . [as on first day].

O happy Rita, who has already crossed over the sea of our mortality, be solicitous toward me in my manifold misery. Reach forth your hands to me, O advocate of desperate cases, and guide my tottering footsteps, that gaining strength through your aid I may walk more confidently in the bypaths of the Savior. Obtain for me faith and perseverance, that I may serve God in fear and so keep His Commandments. I beseech you, O holy Rita, to send me from your home in Heaven a few drops of the wine of your charity, for my soul is dry with the dryness of the world and its pleasures. Come to me, a miserable sinner, and loose the bonds of my captivity. Take me apart from the world-maddened crowds, that I may sit with you and God Almighty, that I may hear the voice of my God breaking in silence to my aching heart.

O glorified Rita, look down upon me still exiled and send me hope and consolation. Obtain for me the grace of imitating your virtues; and if it be God's Holy Will, I beg of you to add your prayers to mine for the obtaining of this, my special request [mention your request].

O Glorious St. Rita, who did miraculously participate in the sorrowful Passion of our Lord Jesus Christ, obtain for me the grace to suffer with resignation the troubles of this life, and protect me in all my needs. *Amen.*

Three each: Our Father, Hail Mary, Glory be.

Litany

of St. Rita of Cascia, O.S.A.

O Blessed St. Rita, our patroness and guide, we lay this chaplet at your feet, a litany, as we do the thoughts, the labors, and the sufferings of our lives, that by holding daily before our eyes the gentle purity, patience, and sanctity of your example our lives may be lived in some poor image of your own, even unto life everlasting.

Lord, have mercy on us. *Christ, have mercy on us.*
Lord, have mercy on us. Christ, hear us. *Christ, graciously hear us.*

God, the Father Almighty, *Have mercy on us.*
God, the Son, Redeemer of the world, who has said: "Ask, and you shall receive; seek, and you shall find; knock, and it shall be opened unto you," . . .
God, the Holy Spirit, Spirit of Wisdom, Understanding, Counsel, and Knowledge, . . .

Holy Trinity, one God, Power Infinite, . . .

Holy Mary, who has never refused those who implored thee, *Pray for us.*

Immaculate Mary, Queen of Heaven and Earth, . . .

Our Lady of the Sacred Heart, . . .

Holy Angels, spirits of humility, . . .

Holy Principalities, charged with the care of religious communities, . . .

Holy Virtues, angels of energy, . . .

Holy Cherubim, angels of light, . . .

St. Rita, advocate of the impossible, . . .

St. Rita, enamored of humility, . . .

St. Rita, consecrated to God, . . .

St. Rita, lover of Jesus crucified, . . .

St. Rita, spouse of Jesus suffering, . . .

St. Rita, penetrated with compassion for our Lord, . . .

St. Rita, crowned by an angel with the sacred crown of thorns, . . .

St. Rita, who did bear the wound of this supernatural coronation upon your forehead, . . .

St. Rita, trusting in the tender mercy of Jesus, . . .

St. Rita, importuning our dying Lord with irresistible fervor, . . .

St. Rita, never doubting the answer to prayer, . . .

That we may renounce all self-love, *Pray for us, St. Rita.*

That we may confide in the promises of Christ, . . .

That the enemies of our salvation may be put to confusion, . . .

That we may accomplish most perfectly the holy will of God, . . .

That the power of evil over us may be destroyed, . . .

That faith may spread in all its purity over our land, . . .

That a holy zeal may take possession of our hearts, . . .

That we may inspire all with whom we associate with a love for holy purity . . .

That we may cultivate a delicate charity in all our actions, . . .

That we may be delivered from all avarice, vainglory, or rash judgment, . . .

That great saints may arise in our nation, to edify the people and enlighten the darkness of infidelity, . . .

That we may be delivered from all interior foes, . . .

Lamb of God, who takes away the sins of the world, *spare us, O Lord.*

Lamb of God, who takes away the sins of the world, *graciously hear us, O Lord.*

Lamb of God, who takes away the sins of the world, *have mercy on us, O Lord.*

Pray for us, St. Rita, *that we may be made worthy of the promises of Christ.*

Let us pray:

O God, who in your infinite tenderness has vouchsafed to regard the prayer of your servant, Blessed Rita, and does grant to her supplication that which is impossible to human foresight, skill, and efforts, in reward for her compassionate love and firm reliance upon your promises, have pity upon our adversity and succor us in our calamities, that the unbeliever may know you are the recompense of the humble, the defense of the helpless, and the strength of those who trust in You. Through Jesus Christ, our Lord. *Amen.*

O Holy Protectress

O HOLY PROTECTRESS of those who are in utmost need, who shines as a star of hope in the midst of darkness, glorious and blessed St. Rita, bright mirror of the Catholic Church, in patience and fortitude as the patriarch Job, scourge of devils, health of the sick, deliverer of those in extreme need, admiration of Saints, and model of all states; with my whole heart and soul prostrated before and firmly united to the adorable will of my God, through the merits of my only Lord and Savior, Jesus Christ, and in particular through the merits of His patient wearing of that torturing crown of thorns, which you, with a tender devotion, did daily contemplate; through the merits of the most sweet Virgin Mary and your own excellent graces and virtues, I implore you to obtain my earnest petition—provided it be for the greater glory of God and my own sanctification [here mention your request], and herein do guide and purify my intention, O holy protectress and most dear advocate, so that I may obtain the pardon of all my sins and grace to persevere, as you did, in walking with courage and generosity and unwavering fidelity through the heavenward path in which the love of my sweet Lord desires to lead me. *Amen.*

Invocations to St. Rita

St. Rita, Advocate of the hopeless, *pray for us.*

St. Rita, Advocate of the Impossible, *pray for us.*

Three each: Our Father, Hail Mary, Glory be.

Blessed be God, the Father of our Lord Jesus Christ, Father of Mercy and God of all Consolation, who, through the intercession of St. Rita, comforts us in all our tribulations. *Amen.*

Novena in Honor of St. Rita

First Day

FROM HER CHILDHOOD, St. Rita had received a wonderful gift of prayer. Like her parents, she was very devout in the practice of her faith. Although she lived an ordinary life, her divine gift was that she was drawn frequently to her parish church, which was her favorite place of prayer and where she spent many hours in prayer and meditation. This gift graced her with the ability to carry her spirit of prayer with her throughout all the ordinary duties and pleasures of life. She continued this practice during her whole life as a wife and mother, but especially after her miraculous entrance into the religious state. Prayer was her life. For not even one moment could she withdraw herself from the presence of her Uncreated Love.

Let prayer, then, be the subject of your thought on the first day of your novena. Frequently recite some prayerful exclamations during the day and ask our Divine Lord in union with the Apostles to teach you how to pray and to fill your heart with the spirit of prayer.

Exercises

Say the Rosary of the Blessed Virgin Mary, the Litany of St. Rita, and the following prayer:

O Blessed Rita, Wonderful model of prayer for those in every state and condition of life, pray to your Divine Spouse, with whom your intercession is so powerful and your prayers so efficacious, that the spirit of prayer may descend into my heart and ever remain there. Obtain for me also, beloved patron, that like you I may find my chief delight in having recourse to my Divine Master; that like you I may be worthy to be numbered among His chosen disciples; that He may protect me during life from the enemies of my soul's salvation and from every danger, and at the moment of my death place me among the heavenly multitude of the blessed. *Amen.*

Then say the prayer "O Holy Protectress," followed by the Invocations to St. Rita.

Second Day

The foundation of every virtue is humility. God
resists the proud and gives His grace to the
humble. Where pride reigns there can be no
virtue. That Rita is the great Saint she is today is
due mainly to the fact of her humility. She
practiced this virtue as a child when she never
tried or wished to prefer herself to anyone. As a
wife she maintained a profound humility. Her
models were Christ Himself, who told His disciples
and followers to learn to be meek and humble of
heart; Mary, the Mother of God, who
notwithstanding that she alone of all the daughters
of Eve was selected to be the Mother of the God-
Man, cried out, "Behold the handmaid of the Lord";
and St John the Baptist, of whom Christ gave the
testimony that he was the greatest born of woman,
who declared himself to be but the "voice of one
crying in the wilderness." In imitation of St. Rita,
then, be humble. Do not feel dejected or
discontented or complain because the world does
not treat you as you think you deserve to be
treated. Do not long for the approval of the
worldly. Frequently today repeat the prayer "Jesus

meek and humble of heart, make my heart like unto Yours."

Exercises

Rosary of the Blessed Virgin, Litany of St. Rita, and the following prayer:

O glorious St. Rita, perfect disciple of the meek and humble Nazarene, because of that most profound humility which you lived every day after being introduced by your holy Protectors, St. John the Baptist, St. Augustine, and St. Nicholas of Tolentino, into the sacred cloister of Cascia through closed doors, where, following the Rule of St. Augustine, you did lead a life hidden with Christ in God, we pray that you obtain for us from that God who resists the proud and imparts His gifts to the humble, the grace to conquer the passion of pride within us, that noxious root of all our woes, so we may become worthy to be raised up to the eternal glory of heaven in imitation of our Divine Redeemer. *Amen.*

Then say the prayer "O Holy Protectress," followed by the Invocations to St. Rita.

Third Day

The Saints were men and women just the same as those now living. They had the same passions, the same temptations as we have. We have the same means and remedies to overcome the great enemies of our salvation—namely the world, the flesh, and the devil—as they had, and yet unfortunately it must be admitted that there is a great difference between the saints and us. The chief cause of this difference is that the saints guided and directed their actions by the spirit of faith. In everything that happened to them they beheld the hand of God and sought His Holy Will. St. Rita had an intense desire to consecrate her life to God in the religious state, but it was only after long years of patient waiting, years filled with suffering and sorrow amid much joy and happiness as a wife and mother, that she was to enjoy the fulfillment of her cherished wish. Yet she was ever cheerful, because she felt these sufferings were permitted by a loving God and she could do nothing more meritorious than submit to His Holy Will.

Let it be our practice during this novena and the remainder of our lives to imitate God's saints, especially our dear St. Rita, in bearing patiently all the adversities of life as allowed by God for our own welfare, and let us repeat frequently the prayer, "Blessed be the Holy Will of God."

Exercises

Rosary of the Blessed Virgin, Litany of St. Rita, and the following prayer:

O glorious St. Rita, chosen friend of Jesus Christ, help me by your intercession and obtain for me the spirit of faith as lively as that which you yourself possessed, that it may guide and direct me in all the adversities of life and teach me to seek in all things the Holy Will of God. May this holy faith lift me above the things of time and show me in accordance with the wisdom of all the saints that I should not place my heart on objects that will so soon pass away, but rather that the only royal road to the kingdom of heaven is the patient endurance of whatever may happen here below. O good Jesus, grant me, through the prayers of St. Rita, the spirit of faith, that glorious gift for which the prince of the Apostles asked with such fervor: "Lord, increase our faith." May my life be in accordance with the teaching of your holy Gospel and may I be able to say with my dying breath, "I have kept the faith" and now am ready for my eternal reward. *Amen.*

Then say the prayer "O Holy Protectress," followed by the Invocations to St. Rita.

Fourth Day

If there was one virtue more than another that distinguished itself in the life of St. Rita, it was her obedience. As a child it was in the light of this virtue that she regulated all her actions. She regarded the slightest wish of her parents as a command of God that she could not violate. It was in obedience to their wish that she, for the time, gave up her ardent desire of becoming a nun and entered marriage. But no sooner had she become a wife than she immediately realized that her duty was to respect and obey her husband with the same reverence that the church owes her head, Christ. It was, however, as a nun that she practiced this virtue to a heroic degree. All her actions were so many acts of obedience, or rather her whole conventual life was an uninterrupted act of the humblest, truest, and readiest obedience.

Learn from St. Rita to prize this holy virtue; be faithful in your observance of the laws of God and His holy Church. Look upon your superiors, whoever they may be, as God's representatives, and in doing their will, as long as it is not sinful, you may be sure you are pleasing God, who one day will reward you as He rewarded St. Rita.

Exercises

Rosary of the Blessed Virgin, Litany of St. Rita, and the following prayer:

O glorious St. Rita, bright ornament of the Augustinian Order; model of obedience during your whole life; perfect disciple of Him who came on earth to do the will of His Heavenly Father, and who was obedient in all things even unto the death of the cross; obtain for me by your powerful intercession the grace to render myself perfectly obedient and submissive to all God's designs in my regard. May I obtain also the grace to behold God in the person of my superiors, spiritual and temporal, and thus render them that loyal and loving service which characterized your every act. Amen.

Then say the prayer "O Holy Protectress," followed by the Invocations to St. Rita.

Fifth Day

In her youth, even while yet a child, Rita's only desire was to consecrate herself to God in the religious state. But alas! What trials and sufferings were to come upon her before she was to experience the joy of this religious consecration. In obedience to her parents' wish, she entered the married state. After the death of her husband and children, when she tried to gain admittance to the convent, she was again refused, more than once, and finally, when enrolled among the nuns of Cascia, she suffered many additional afflictions. Yet in all these trials, great indeed though they were and lasting her whole life, she was never known to utter a word of complaint. Rather, hers was ever a peaceful and joyous countenance, and on her lips was a word of comfort for every sufferer who came in contact with her. Well did she learn the patience and resignation of her beloved Master.

You too, her devoted client, be sure to imitate these special virtues and you may be certain that as God rewarded St. Rita, so too will He bless you. Remember that every pain, no matter how slight, if it be borne with patience, will become a jewel of infinite price in your crown of glory.

Exercises

Rosary of the Blessed Virgin, Litany of St. Rita, and the following prayer:

O blessed Rita, model of patience and resignation to the will of God in all your trials; how much I need the consolation afforded by meditating on your sufferings and learning from you never to be downcast but always to raise my eyes to heaven, there seeking as you did the strength to bear patiently the various ills of life. Obtain for me from your Divine Spouse and Model those virtues of patience and resignation, the true philosophers' stone, which will change the ordinary trials of life into the precious pearls of a glorious diadem, similar to that which now adorns your brow, and which will be forever yours in reward for your patiently bearing the cross your heavenly Father sent you. *Amen.*

Then say the prayer "O Holy Protectress," followed by the Invocations to St. Rita.

Sixth Day

The constant object of St. Rita's thoughts during her whole life, and which caused the ecstasies of her soul as well as the most ardent love of her heart, was the Passion of her Crucified Spouse. She felt herself absorbed into the Crucified One, for whom alone she lived. To Him she poured out the loving longings of her heart, that all might do homage to the Son of God, who out of love suffered such torments for them. One day, fifteen years before her death, while contemplating an image of Jesus crowned with thorns, she asked to relieve the sufferings of her beloved Lord. She was rewarded with the wound of a thorn in her forehead, a source of pain but also a sign of love, which she bore faithfully until her death.

Dear client of St. Rita, there is no form of meditation simpler or more advantageous than meditation on the sorrowful Passion of Christ. Let it be your chief delight, with St. Rita, in whose honor you are making this Novena, to dwell with loving thoughts on this Sacred Passion, especially today. Think of it during your work, your free time, and ask St. Rita, to obtain for you the same delights from this holy exercise as inundated her pure soul.

Exercises

Rosary of the Blessed Virgin, Litany of St. Rita, and the following prayer:

> O sweet Lord Jesus, Who became man for the salvation of the human race, and who suffered such untold pains and humiliations that guilty man might be restored again to the love and friendship of his Creator, grant that through the merits of blessed Rita the sorrows of Your Passion may be the constant object of my thoughts and aspirations. Imprint deeply in my heart the love of Your Passion, and grant that in imitation of my glorious patron, St. Rita, I may deserve to hear an answer to my prayers and may come with her to eternal happiness. *Amen.*

Then say the prayer "O Holy Protectress," followed by the Invocations to St. Rita.

Seventh Day

Forgiveness of injuries is a duty incumbent on every Christian who claims to be a follower of Christ. The necessity of this duty is taught not only by the positive precepts of our Divine Lord, but far more forcibly by the example of His life, for when hanging on the Cross His dying words were a prayer to His heavenly Father for the pardon of His murderers, "Father, forgive them, for they know not what they do." So thoroughly was St. Rita convinced of the necessity of pardoning her enemies, and so desirous was she of imitating the example of her beloved Spouse that she did not for a moment hesitate to pardon sincerely from her heart the cruel men who brutally murdered her unfortunate husband. She too, in imitation of the example of the dying Redeemer, offered fervent supplications to the divine mercy for those wicked murderers.

We, the clients of St. Rita, wishing to honor her and obtain her protection during this novena, should bear continually in mind that there is no better way to ensure her help than by a fervent and loyal imitation of her virtues.

Resolve then today to banish from your heart all ill will and uncharitable feelings toward those who may have done you any injury. Forgive, and as you deal with others, so will your heavenly Father deal with you, for charity covers a multitude of sins.

Exercises

Rosary of the Blessed Virgin, Litany of St. Rita, and the following prayer:

O dearest Lord, how many times I have offended You and how kind you have been to me in granting me the grace of repentance. I acknowledge that my life has been one of ingratitude for the numberless favors You have bestowed upon me. I thank you especially for the various lessons of virtue you have given to me through the life of blessed Rita, and I beg of You to impress on my heart the lesson of forgiveness of injuries. O blessed Rita, spouse of Jesus suffering, you who were so cruelly treated by others during life and yet pardoned from your inmost heart the injuries you received, obtain for me the favor to love all men, even those who may do me the greatest injuries. *Amen.*

Then say the prayer "O Holy Protectress," followed by the Invocations to St. Rita.

Eighth Day

St. Rita, one of the greatest saints whom God has been pleased to raise up in modern times, may be truly considered a model for every condition in life, as well as a bright exemplar of the virtues that ought to adorn every good and fervent Christian. Holy Church has solemnly declared that she practiced these virtues to a heroic degree. However, there is one practice that in her holy life stands out more prominently than all the others, and that is her love and devotion toward Jesus in the Holy Eucharist. As a child she spent much time in church devoted to prayer. As a wife and mother her chief delight was to receive into her loving heart the Divine Spouse of her soul. As a nun she spent much time in prayer before the Tabernacle. Yet no matter what duties she was called on to perform, her affections were ever directed to that sacred spot where her treasure was.

O dear client of St. Rita, learn from her that no devotion is of any account that does not bring you into closer contact with the Most Blessed Sacrament. Receive it frequently and worthily.

Exercises

Rosary of the Blessed Virgin, Litany of St. Rita, and the following prayer:

> O sweet Lord Jesus, who out of love for me remains day and night in the Most Holy Sacrament of the Altar, often lonely and neglected by those You love, but more so by me, O grant me, dear Jesus, through the intercession of Your beloved servant Rita, to find my joy and consolation in visiting You in this Sacrament and in receiving You into my heart. I desire now to receive You but, alas, I am not prepared. Come then into my soul in spirit. Prepare it for that happy moment when I will have the happiness of receiving You sacramentally as the crowning work of this novena, and grant me, through the intercession of St. Rita, the favors I am asking of You during these days of prayer. *Amen.*

Then say the prayer "O Holy Protectress," followed by the Invocations to St. Rita.

Ninth Day

Coming near the end of her holy and miraculous life, St. Rita felt she was languishing with love for her heavenly bridegroom. This love was the characteristic of her pure life, the guiding principle of her every act, and now, in her last moments on Earth, it caused her to desire her freedom from the ties of her body so that she might take her flight to enjoy for all eternity her Uncreated Good. Our Divine Lord, accompanied by His Most Holy Mother, appeared to her and announced the joyous tidings that she would be taken from this world and all her pains and be received into Paradise to receive the reward of her virtues and sufferings. With what fervor did she immediately prepare to receive them, a fervor more easily imagined than described, and then, with her eyes turned toward the abode of the blessed, her pure soul took its flight to heaven,

where she now lives an immortal life, the reward
of her heroic virtues.

Her precious death took place on the night of
May 22, 1457, the last day of the week, a day
specially consecrated to the honor of the Mother of
God, whom, after God Himself, she loved with her
whole heart. Be devoted to Mary, and ask her
frequently to intercede for you at the hour of your
death.

Exercises

Rosary of the Blessed Virgin, Litany of St. Rita, and
the following prayer:

> O glorious St. Rita, filled with love for your
> heavenly Father, take me today, unworthy
> though I be, under your powerful
> protection, and obtain for me the favor I am
> seeking during this novena [mention your
> request]. I beseech you also to obtain for me
> the ineffable grace of loving God with my
> whole heart during the remainder of my
> life, of loving Him above all things in
> imitation of the bright example of your life,

that thus I may merit as you did to die in the sweet embrace of Jesus and Mary. O teach me, dear Saint, to prepare myself for that moment on which so much depends, and obtain that death may be for me the entrance to eternal life. *Amen.*

Then say the prayer "O Holy Protectress," followed by the Invocations to St. Rita.

Acknowledgments

SPECIAL THANKS TO THE Augustinian Fathers of 1914; Michael DiGregorio, O.S.A.; Deborah Binder, Director of Development at the National Shrine of St. Rita, Philadelphia, PA; the Dominican Sisters of the Perpetual Rosary, Lancaster, PA; Janice and Patrick Russoniello, Thomas C. Russoniello, Joan P. Russoniello, Diane Grabowski, Jeanette Sexton, Maureen Griesser, Margaret Propst, Brenda Asso, Adele Ruszak, and Kathy Haddon; St. Rita's Church, Baltimore, MD; the loving prayers of Rose Pezonosky and the St. John Neumann Church Rosary Group, Lancaster, PA; and the generous financial support and prayers of the World Apostolate of Our Lady of Fatima Prayer Cell from St. Leo the Great Roman Catholic Church, Rohrerstown, PA.

Made in the USA
Monee, IL
11 May 2023